Kaori
and the
Lizard King

Robert Campbell & Piet Peterson

STARTER
LEVEL

SCHOLASTIC

Material written by: Robert Campbell
Special thanks to Lindsay Clandfield

Commissioning Editor: Jacquie Bloese

Editor: Carolyn Barraclough

Cover design: Dawn Wilson

Designer: Dawn Wilson

Picture research: Emma Bree

Photo credits:
Page 26: Mary Glasgow Magazines.
Page 27: BVI/Everett/Rex Features; AMPAS/AFP/Getty
Images. **Pages 28 & 29:** Disney/BVI; AFP/Getty Images; New
Line, E. Wing/Rex Features.

Illustrations: Piet Peterson

Mary Glasgow Magazines (Scholastic Ltd.)
Euston House
24 Eversholt Street
London
NW1 1DB

Printed in Singapore. Reprinted in 2008.
This edition printed in 2009.

Contents | Page

Kaori and the Lizard King — 4–25

People and places — 4

Kaori and the Lizard King — 6–25

Fact Files — 26–29

Manga facts — 26

Fantasy worlds — 28

Self-Study Activities — 29–32

New Words! — see inside back cover

Kaori and the Lizard King

KAORI

Kaori is 13. She goes to Lucertola High School. She's in love with Jeff.

LUCERTOLA

Lucertola is a beautiful island. There are lots of beaches on the island and one mountain, Mount Oscurola.

There are lots of lizards on the island, but not many children.

Lucertola is very hot and it doesn't rain very often. There isn't much water. Why? Something is happening...

Mount Oscurola

Lucertola

JEFF

Jeff also goes to Lucertola High School. He's in Kaori's class.

SIM-PAT

Sim-Pat is a lizard, but he can talk!

Hi!

TEACHER

Kaori's teacher is very clever. She knows lots of things.

THE LIZARD KING

Who or what is he? No-one knows.

Kaori and the Lizard King

It's Monday morning on the island of Lucertola and Kaori is at school.

LUCERTOLA HIGH SCHOOL

Today Kaori is learning about her country.

DO YOU REMEMBER THE NAME OF THE MOUNTAIN ON OUR ISLAND?

KAORI?

But Kaori isn't listening. She's thinking about Jeff, a boy in her class.

KAORI!

I LOVE YOU, JEFF. I LOVE YOUR EYES, YOUR HAIR... DO YOU LOVE ME, JEFF?

After the class Kaori sees the teacher.

VERY GOOD, KAORI!

BUT REMEMBER: WAIT FOR THE RIGHT TIME BEFORE YOU USE YOUR POWERS.

WHEN IS THE RIGHT TIME?

WHEN I TELL YOU.

I KNOW YOUR FRIEND JEFF.

YOU'RE WRONG. I CAN HELP YOU.

HOW? WHERE IS HE?

ON THE MOUNTAIN?

NOT **ON** THE MOUNTAIN — **IN** THE MOUNTAIN.

IN MOUNT OSCUROLA? I DON'T UNDERSTAND.

LISTEN TO MY STORY...

IT'S A DARK NIGHT... A BOY IS CRYING FOR HELP...

HELP!!!

It's night and Kaori and Sim-Pat climb the mountain.

*Your majesty: *you say this to a king*

MANGA

Kaori and the Lizard King is like a manga comic book.
What is manga? Here are ten facts about manga.

1 Manga comes from Japan.

2 In Japanese manga means "comic book".

3 Girls and boys in many countries love these comics.

4 Manga comics are more than 65 years old. The idea comes from 200-year-old Japanese pictures.

What do these words mean? You can look in a dictionary.

comic   hero/heroes   film

26

FACTS

Howl's Moving Castle

5 You read Japanese manga books from right to left and not left to right.

6 There are different manga comics for boys and girls. *Shonen* manga is for boys and *Shojo* manga is for girls.

7 Stories in manga comics can be two or three years long!

8 One famous manga by Osamu Tezuka has 3,000 pages.

Spirited Away

9 The heroes of manga stories are usually teenagers. They have special powers but they don't always know this.

10 The name for manga films like *Spirited Away*, is *anime*.

Make a Manga

Do you like manga? Look at the picture of Kaori. Can you draw her picture?
Take a pencil and some paper. Look at her head. Now look at her hair, her eyes, nose and mouth.
Is your picture good?
Now draw a manga picture of a friend!

FANTASY

Lucertola is not a real place. It's a fantasy world. There are many famous fantasy worlds. Read about these fantasy worlds and answer these questions:

1. Where do children never grow old?
2. Where can animals talk?
3. Who grows tall and then grows small?
4. Who has a ring?

Narnia

The Lion, the Witch and the Wardrobe is one of seven fantasy stories in *The Chronicles of Narnia* by C. S. Lewis. In the fantasy world of Narnia, animals can talk and there is lots of magic.

The Lion, the Witch and the Wardrobe is now a film. In the story, four children find a door to Narnia inside a wardrobe. They find a new world. It's always winter there. They meet Aslan the lion. He helps them and they fight the White Witch. Winter ends.

What do these words mean? You can look in a dictionary.
fantasy   fight   magic   winter   world

Main picture: *The Lion, the Witch and the Wardrobe*, 2005

WORLDS

Neverland

Neverland is the fantasy island in J. M. Barrie's story of *Peter Pan*. In the story, Wendy and her brothers go with Peter to Neverland. In Neverland, children never grow old.

The children live on the island with the Lost Boys, Indians, Captain Hook, and his pirates. In the film *Finding Neverland*, Johnny Depp is J.M. Barrie, the writer.

Finding Neverland, 2003

Middle-Earth

Middle-Earth is the fantasy world of *The Lord of the Rings* by J. R. R. Tolkien. It is Britain's favourite book – and it's very long!

The story of *The Lord of the Rings* starts with a birthday party for Frodo Baggins. Frodo is a Hobbit. Hobbits are not the same as people. They are smaller. In the story, Frodo has a magic Ring. He wears the Ring and people can't see him. The actor Elijah Wood is Frodo in the film.

Lord of the Rings, 2001

Wonderland

In *Alice's Adventures in Wonderland* by Lewis Carroll, a girl follows a rabbit into a fantasy world. In Wonderland, Alice grows tall and then grows small. She meets a baby. It changes into a pig and a cat. And she drinks tea at a party that never ends. Wonderland is a magic place where animals can talk. At the end of the story Alice goes back to the real world.

Alice in Wonderland, 1972

Can you find these words in the pictures?

grow small   ring   wardrobe

Pages 1–5: At School

Before you read

1 Make parts of the body with the letters.
- **a)** seey
- **b)** rahi
- **c)** homut
- **d)** seno
- **e)** teef

2 Match these words to make useful phrases.
- **a)** Very .... to me.
- **b)** Thank .... ready?
- **c)** Do you .... good.
- **d)** Listen .... remember?
- **e)** Are you .... you.

3 Match the questions with the answers.
- **a)** What are you listening to?
- **b)** Are you happy?
- **c)** Who are you thinking about?
- **d)** What are you learning at school?
- **e)** Do you remember the answer?

- **i)** Yes, I do.
- **ii)** My brother.
- **iii)** The radio.
- **iv)** Yes, I am.
- **v)** English.

After you read

4 True or false?
- **a)** Lucertola is an island.
- **b)** It's Saturday morning.
- **c)** Jeff is a teacher.
- **d)** Mount Oscurola is a mountain.
- **e)** Kaori has a secret.

5 Put these sentences in the correct order.
- **a)** Kaori: I don't want to be different.
- **b)** Teacher: It's time. Are you ready?
- **c)** Kaori: Why can't I love him?
- **d)** Teacher: But you are different. And you can't tell Jeff. It's a secret.
- **e)** Kaori: Yes.
- **f)** Teacher: Listen to me, Kaori. You can't love Jeff.
- **g)** Kaori: I don't like secrets.
- **h)** Teacher: Because you're different.

Pages 6–11: On the Road

Before you read

6 Complete the sentences using one of the words.

hungry   **sad**   **hot**   **tired**

a) I'm _____. I want to sleep.

b) Can we eat? I'm very _____.

c) I'm _____ because the holidays are ending.

d) It's a sunny day and I'm _____.

7 Match the two halves of the sentences.

a) The car   **i)** is running onto the road.

b) The small boy   **ii)** my friend.

c) I'm looking for   **iii)** next to the teacher.

d) They're sitting   **iv)** is going very fast.

After you read

8 Choose the correct preposition.

in   **down**   **in**   **into**   **onto**

a) Kaori walks _____ the road.

b) Sim Pat runs _____ the road.

c) Sim Pat says Jeff is _____ the mountain.

d) In Sim Pat's story, the boy is _____ the lorry.

e) The boy changes _____ a lizard.

9 Answer these questions.

a) What does Kaori hear on the road?

b) Can Sim Pat help Kaori?

c) In Sim-Pat's story, where does the boy go?

d) What do the big lizards give the boy?

e) What happens when the boy drinks?

f) Who is the boy in the story?

Pages 12–20: In the Mountain

Before you read

10 Which of these nouns is not a person?

    a) mother   **b)** father   **c)** lizard

    d) teacher   **e)** boy   **f)** girl

11 Put the verbs into the correct sentences.

    a) changing   **i)** I have a story to _____ you.

    b) has   **ii)** I can't _____ the window.

    c) is raining   **iii)** Look! He _____ big feet.

    d) open   **iv)** It _____ today!

    e) tell   **v)** I'm _____ my clothes because I'm hot.

After you read

12 What do these comic words describe?

    a) HA HA HA!

    b) CRACK! WHACK!

    c) AAAAAAARGH!

    d) WHOOSH!

    i) Kaori, Jeff and Sim-Pat flying off for a new adventure.

    ii) Kaori, Jeff and Sim-Pat hitting the Lizard King.

    iii) The Lizard King laughing.

    iv) The Lizard King feeling angry.

13 What do you think?

    a) Is it good to share secrets?

    b) Which is your favourite character?

    c) What do you think happens in Kaori's new adventure?